Parenting with a Focus on Family

Keys to Impacting the Next Generation

Kyle Strachan

Published by:
Ellis & Ellis Consulting Group, LLC
P.O. Box 938802 Margate, FL 33063
www.ellisandellisconsulting.org

Copyright © 2021. Kyle Strachan

Printed in the United States of America.

Dedication

This book is dedicated to those who I have been touched by through friendships, acquaintances, work colleagues and family. I am forever grateful for the lessons taught, and the many experiences learned. But most importantly, I am forever indebted to those past and present who impacted my life in ways I cannot describe.

Acknowledgements

To my hardworking father who has provided leadership, stability and showed me a work ethic second to none. Thank you, for leading by example.

To my mother who from the time I was a small child insisted that I read, read and read. You showered me with books and other reading material and exposed me to different styles of writing, and ways of thinking. At an early age, you provided me with a means and an avenue to express myself. I am forever indebted to you for the foundation that you provided.

This finished work would not have been possible without the direction of Dr. Lucile Richardson. Thank you for providing mentorship, encouragement and inspiration from the first day we met. I am forever grateful.

Table of Contents

Parenting with a Focus on Family

Keys to Impacting the Next Generation

INTRODUCTION

"Problems cannot be solved by the same level of thinking that created them."

--Albert Einstein

Today's traditional families are defined by the basic building block of a society that provides structure and sets core values for parenting the next generation. However, society has become very complex and intertwined with a variety of values; while some have no values at all. With any approach comes a new way of thinking in order to achieve beneficial results.

Many parents are departing from traditional ways of thinking and parenting while adapting to change. Mahatma Gandhi says, "We must become the change we want to see." Parents must first see the change in order to be the change, which entails taking on a whole new vision for some, and for others it means adding to the already changing vision and concept of parenthood starting with the parent.

This book focuses on family and parenting. Many references are made about children and adolescents. You will find that some of the basic principles used to train adolescents can be applied to parenting all children. The goal is for readers to consider a different way of thinking and to bring about a paradigm shift. It is not about people but the things God has established to help guide them in every aspect of parenting.

By no means does this book provide a mandatory list of how parenting should be done. My aim is to provide keys that will help parents in their parenting while impacting the next generation.

CHAPTER 1

GOD'S PURPOSE
FOR FAMILY

"In the home begins the disruption of the
peace of the world."

--Mother Teresa

Genesis 12:3, God told Abraham: *"... And in you all the families (nations) of the earth will be blessed."* He further states in Genesis 18:19, *"For I have known (chosen, acknowledged) him [Abraham] [as My own] so that he may teach and command his children and the sons of his house after him to keep the way of the LORD and to do what is just and righteous, so the LORD may bring Abraham what He has promised him"* (Genesis 18:19, Amplified Bible). Galatians 3:29 says, *"And if you belong to Christ [if you are in Him], then you are Abraham's descendants, and [spiritual] heirs according to [God's] promise."*

God has a plan and a purpose for everything in life. Nothing is done without being in fulfillment of His intent. We were created to fulfill His purpose and glorify His name forever. This purpose for life also applies to marriage, including the reason for getting married.

The ultimate purpose of marriage is spiritual—not physical, emotional, or social. Each new marriage forms a new spiritual entity or partnership—a family—that has spiritual responsibilities to God and to society. The family is to serve as the first channel of God's blessings and revelations, a place where he can establish a direct contact and relationship with each one of the family members, including the children. In other words, the family is expected to provide the following needs of its members so they can become productive and useful for God and His work on Earth:

- Physical;
- Emotional;
- Social;
- Economic; and
- Spiritual.

FOUR CRITICAL PURPOSES FOR GOD'S FAMILY

God outlines the critical purposes for His family in Genesis 1:26-28 (New International Version): *"Then God said, "Let us make mankind in our image, in our likeness, so that they may rule over the fish in the sea and the birds in the sky, over the livestock and all the wild animals, and over all the creatures that move along the ground." So God created mankind in his own image, in the image of God he created them; male and female he created them. God blessed them and said to them, "Be fruitful and increase in number; fill the earth and subdue it. Rule over the fish in the sea and the birds in the sky and over every living creature that moves on the ground."*

This passage reveals four critical purposes for God's family:
1. To reflect the image of God.
2. To conduct Government.
3. To produce and raise a godly heritage.
4. To nurture God's people.

1. To Reflect the Image of God

God first created the universe, the Earth, and all plant and animal life. Afterwards, He then created a new creation; He created human beings, different from all the rest in one very important point, (Genesis 1:26) *"Let us make humans in Our image according to Our likeness."* God Himself breathed the *"breath of life"* into man's nostrils and he became a *"living soul"* (Genesis 2:7). By this act, God imparted to humans a little piece of Himself, thereby lifting man from the condition of being a mere transient body, into the state of being a permanent, part-physical, part-spiritual creation.

As a spiritual being, man is thus able to communicate with and relate to God. In fact, he is required to. The Psalmist asks the question, *"What is man that you are mindful of him, the son of man that you visit him? For you made him a little lower than the angels, and you have crowned him with glory and Honor. You made him to have dominion over the works of your hands; you have put all things under his feet..."* (Psalm 8:4-6). Man, because of his physical body, is a "little lower than the angels," who are only spiritual. But he is not as low as the animals, which are only physical. Thus, man is a one-of-a-kind, in-between creature, a spiritualized body.

Included in the image of God is the ability to possess the attributes of God. This includes emotions like love, joy, peace, security, kindness, and other positive, God-like qualities. It also includes the possession of superior intelligence, curiosity, complex desires, the need for companionship and relationships, the need to find meaning in life, to worship something somewhere, etc.

God Himself is a God of love and light, and He wants us to reflect His love and light in this world. This is especially true now that sin has broken the spiritual connection man had with God, and the world is now filled with darkness. The family also reflects the image of God in its structure.

A properly-formed family is not just a woman who chooses to have a baby and raise it on her own. A proper family consists of three necessary ingredients: a husband, a wife, and God as the ultimate Head. We know that unfortunate circumstances arise all the time, often beyond a person's control, that prevent the proper formation and functioning of a family, and in such cases the single parent should learn to lean very heavily on God, their family and the church family for support. Still, everyone involved, including society, is impacted when any of these three basic ingredients of a proper family are missing.

2. To Conduct Government

The second purpose of the family is to conduct government for God's intention, which is for humans to have dominion over all of the rest of His earthly creation in order to bring everything into harmony with Him and His will. This concept is repeated throughout the Bible—in Genesis, in Psalm 8:6 and Hebrews 2:7-8, *"You made him to have dominion over the works of Your hands; You have put all things under his feet", to name a few.*

Human beings possess the image of God and many of His abilities. They are the only creation on earth capable of having dominion. It is therefore incumbent upon man to set all of God's creation in order: to build government and maintain order, to develop civilization, to organize earthly efforts, to harness the power and abilities of the rest of creation, etc.

In Genesis chapter 2, Adam began fulfilling his commission to "have dominion" in the Garden of Eden. However, he did not have adequate tools. He needed a "helper fitting or suitable for him" (Genesis 2:18). Thus, 'woman' was created, and the concept of marriage and family began.

Some special qualities that are to come through the family include the concepts of love, acceptance of others, placing a high value on life, self-esteem, security, morality, peace, justice, mercy, liberty, self-denial for the good of others, and protection of the rights of the individual. These things are learned best within the structure of a strong family.

More importantly, the family is to impart and perpetuate the experiential knowledge of God. Thus, if the family, for any reason, is prevented from producing people who possess these special qualities, the whole society suffers. Society, the government, and the average person may be motivated by selfishness, and selfishness is always self-destructive. History has shown that any society ruled by selfishness eventually collapses upon itself.

3.   **To Produce and Raise a Godly Heritage**

One of the most important purposes of the family is to raise a Godly heritage to fill the Earth with God-fearing, morally mature, emotionally sound, righteousness-working, God-worshiping young people, who in turn, will do the same after they become parents. God's desire is that parents would concentrate on building character and a Godly spirit into their children. His desire is that His people would extend a Godly heritage throughout the present world and down through the coming generations.

Here are a few scriptures regarding children:

"Didn't the Lord make you one with your wife? In body and spirit you are his. And what does He want? Godly children from your union. So guard yourself; remain loyal to the wife of your youth." (Malachi 2:15, New Living Translation).

"Lo, children are an heritage of the LORD: and the fruit of the womb is his reward. As arrows are in the hand of a mighty man; so are children of the youth. Happy is the man that hath his quiver full of them..." (Psalm 127:3-5, King James Version).

"I will open my mouth in a parable: I will utter dark sayings of old: Which we have heard and known, and our fathers have told us. We will not hide them from their children, showing to the generation to come the praises of the LORD, and his strength, and his wonderful works that he hath done. For he established a testimony in Jacob, and appointed a law in Israel, which he commanded our fathers, that they should make them known to their children: That the generation to come might know them, even the children which should be born; who should arise and declare them to their children: That they might set their hope in God, and not forget the works of God, but keep his commandments." (Psalm 78:2-7, King James Version).

"For the promise is unto you, and to your children, and to all that are afar off, even as many as the Lord our God shall call." (Acts 2:39, King James Version).

From these passages we get God's perspective on the family with regards to children. In the first scripture, Genesis 12:3, the concept that the ultimate purpose of a righteous family is to "bless" all of the other families in the earth is clearly introduced. Malachi 2:15 contains another very interesting concept. It is also a very challenging concept in our world of today, where marriage and having children are increasingly disassociated from each other. More and more marriages are childless for a variety of reasons, and more and more children exist outside of wedlock. The prophet asks: *"Didn't the Lord make you one with your wife? In body and spirit you are his. And what does He want? Godly children from your union."*

A similar reading comes from the Contemporary English Version (CEV): *"Didn't God create you to become like one person with your wife? And why did he do this? It was so you would have children, and then lead them to become God's people. Don't ever be unfaithful to your wife."* Many translations give exactly the same message.

Here is God's meaning in plain English: Your spirit is mine, and your body is mine because I made you. I also created marriage, where you could find love and happiness and physical pleasure with another human being and still be in My will. In other words, under holiness and the Lordship of Jesus Christ, God Himself claims to be the ruler over our "reproductive rights and powers."

4. To Nurture God's People

The fourth critical purpose for the family is to serve as the nurturer of people. Parents must nurture their children especially adolescents who will certainly seek it outside the family if not received. God designed human beings to live and be kind to each other instead of fighting like animals. It is our nurturing nature that energizes heaven and earth.

In all creation, humans appear to be the one species that cannot thrive without nurturing relationships. Therefore, one of the most important purposes of the family is to nurture God's people throughout their lives. God sent Jesus Christ into the world, to bring us the love and acceptance that He made us crave, so we can nurture the next generation; we will never completely find other species nurturing their offspring throughout their life.

Children victimized by families that are dysfunctional, abusive, neglecting and collapsing may substitute their need to be nurtured through seeking love, money, power, fame, etc. They may compensate by destroying themselves with negative Behaviors powered by low self-esteem. Or they may lose themselves in non-productive romantic relationships leading to promiscuity, teen pregnancy, cohabitation, serial marriages, etc. They may try drowning out their pain with drugs, alcohol, sex, deviant pleasures, and other addictions.

Even at their best, people are affected in subtle ways that they may never even realize: fears, insecurities, mistrust, low self-esteem, pessimism, possessiveness, being over sensitive, and other emotional weaknesses.

Therefore, families must concentrate more on building and nurturing people—both within and without the family. However, nurturing people is not one of the top priorities in today's world, not even in many Christian families. For some reason, many families seem to aim most of their thoughts and efforts on materialistic goals, and forget all about nurturing each other. Many parents seem to focus most of their efforts on their own desires, careers, comfort, and personal fulfillment, failing to make the nurturing of their children and spouses to be their chief duty in life. Society continues to reap the negative results of such selfish practices.

Whatever the situation may be, the fact remains that both parents are required to concentrate on their family responsibilities as their most important duties in life. In order to fulfill their family's special calling, nothing in life is more important than the building of strong character, the development of noble social graces, the fulfillment of all emotional needs, and the successful spiritual connecting of every young heart to its Maker. All of this must be done within the family, by parents who concentrate on their individual primary purposes and roles. Anything less may result in gravely ill families and societies in today's world.

Many social institutions around us—marriage, family, schools, government, business—are becoming increasingly dysfunctional, and in the throes of collapsing. The rate of crimes committed by young people is increasing. Many people blame the government and leaders. But perhaps we need to first take another look inside our homes to see what can be done better before we condemn the government, leaders and even school teachers for not doing enough.

Mother Teresa said, *"In the home begins the disruption of the peace of the world."*

CHAPTER 2

ESSENTIAL DIMENSIONS
OF PARENTING

From the birth of a child, the reality of parenting and the challenges in life that lie ahead become a certainty. The baby is seen as an adorable little warm teddy bear loved by everyone. At this stage, parents try to establish a bond that will last for a life time. They sing and read books, becoming playmates; but most importantly, they become caretakers. Around the second year of the child's life these attributes are still present, however more emphasis is placed on teaching the child how to behave or how not to behave. (Fagot & Kavanaugh, 1993), (Shaffer, 1999, p.564)

Researchers such as Erikson (Macoby & Martin, 1983) have indicated that there are two essential dimensions of parenting throughout childhood and adolescence. They are as follows:

1. Parental Acceptance/Responsiveness
2. Parental Demandingness/Control

1. Parental Acceptance/Responsiveness

Essentially parental acceptance/responsiveness focuses on the amount of love and support that is demonstrated by parents. Some parents express an overwhelming amount of love and warmth. However, at times they can be very critical if the child misbehaves (Shaffer, 1999, p.564). Their emotions trigger them to engage their children. An emotional trigger stems from something said to someone which stirs up an emotion that can affect interaction and communication between parent and child.

Parental acceptance, or parental responsiveness shapes the interaction between parent and child. At an early age, this type of parenting fosters child socialization. Children need to be able to comfortably express themselves through communication; it is necessary in any relationship. Acceptance/responsiveness provides children with emotional and mental stability engrained in them for a lifetime.

2. Parental Demandingness/Control

This dimension of parenting focuses on the amount of regulation that parents undertake with their children (Shaffer, 1999, p.565). In the case of a controlling or demanding parent, a child's freedom of expression is limited and in some cases restricted. The parent constantly monitors the child's behavior by ensuring that their rules and regulations are followed and respected. This type of parenting can be very overwhelming for children. However children do need to be controlled and regulated while being guided by wisdom. This fosters good parenting as rules are needed to ensure that children behave and follow instructions.

Parents must understand how and when to limit a child's freedom of expression, because limiting the freedom of expression can bring about an authoritarian style of parenting and build resentment within a child. Limiting a child's freedom of expression is not good for child socialization as children have a right and a need to express themselves. When this style is implemented correctly it fosters good communication, interaction, discipline and socialization. In contrast, non-controlling parents are less restrictive. They have fewer demands and allow children the freedom to navigate and pursue their interests and decisions about their own activities (Shaffer, 1999, p.565).

Diana Baumrind's research on the two dimensions of parenting cited four styles that are related to those styles. (Baumrind, 1973; 1991), (Siegler et al., 2003, p.457), (Shaffer, 1999, p.565).

1.   Authoritarian
2.   Authoritative
3.   Permissive
4.   Uninvolved

1.   Authoritarian Parenting

In Authoritarian Parenting (Shaffer, 1999, p.565), parents expect a child to accept whatever they say and respect their authority. There are many rules and little room to ask questions. The parent is insensitive to the child's views and the margin between compliance and finding an alternative solution is slim. One may say at what age is a child allowed to ask questions? An Authoritarian parent may say the child is allowed to ask questions when he or she allows them to.

However, parents should communicate the reason for their actions and what made them come to their conclusion. Parents should communicate to their children early in life about how their actions cause certain consequences. They should explain or state their reasons for not wanting the child to do something e.g. to go outside and play,

2. Authoritative Parenting

This approach is flexible, yet controlling; however, the parent's demands are reasonable. These parents provide alternative solutions and they justify their actions and reasons about why they set limits and boundaries. Authoritative parents are receptive and responsive to the views of their children and usually involve them in the family decision-making process. Children have greater autonomy within the limits set by the parents. A parent knows when their child is ready to offer opinions (which parents take seriously) and they know when to involve them in the decision making process. This form of parenting is good but children can feel overwhelmed by an authoritative parent; therefore, there must be a balance between being authoritative and receptive. Being too authoritative can result in children not wanting to communicate or express themselves to parents.

3. Permissive Parenting

This approach is less monitored and children are able to express their views, feelings and impulses (Shaffer, 1999, p.566). It can be seen as an accepting but lackadaisical style of parenting as there are few demands by parents and less control over the child's behavior. Initially, this form of parenting may seem great but because children are children they need to be controlled, especially when it relates to their behavior. Some children's behavior is a reflection of the parents and their parenting skills. If a child is unruly and disrespectful at a young age, it is usually because the parent fails to correct and discipline the child. This parenting style has no rules, laws or boundaries. The child simply does what they want when they want. When children become teenagers or adults and enter society, sometimes they feel like they can get away with whatever they got away with at home. Because of this parenting style, sometimes children end up on the wrong side of the law, stuck in drug abuse; or they meet their untimely demise from their lifestyle and choices. However, if parents begin to set rules and boundaries when children are young, as they mature they will have a foundation and better understanding of how to behave, show respect and obey the law.

4.   Uninvolved Parenting

This style of parenting is where the responsiveness and demand of the parent are minimal (Shaffer, 1999, p.567). The approach is very laid-back and displayed by parents who have either rejected or given up on their children, or they may be encapsulated by their own stress and problems and as a result, they do not have time to devote to the children (Macoby & Martin, 1983), (Shaffer, 1999, p.567). *"At age [three] children of uninvolved parents are… relatively high in aggression and portray temper tantrums"* (Miller et al., 1993). Later in childhood this child's academic ability is poor (Eckenrode, Laird, & Doris, 1993) (Shaffer, 1999, p.567). Far too often children of uninvolved parents become rebellious, ill-tempered and lack goals. They engage in drug abuse, sexual misconduct and even criminal offences (Lamborn et al., 1991; Kurdek & Fine, 1994; Patterson et al., 1992; Weiss & Schwarz, 1996) (Shaffer 1999, p.565).

Many children who feel unwanted or unimportant because of rejection from their parents usually blame themselves. Instead of blaming their parents they think they are the problem. They feel lonely and left out, and as a result they seek attention from friends and anyone else. Their antisocial behavior can result from parents not being involved enough in their lives. This kind of parenting can foster rebellious and disrespectful children who lack a sense of direction. It can be bad for parents who may feel they have failed their children by not training and giving them a good foundation either mentally, emotionally, or spiritually.

THE EFFECTS OF PARENTING STYLES

Parenting styles may have serious effects on the developmental outcome of children and adolescents. The style of parenting is intertwined and interconnected with a child's educational performance, social behavior and mental health, at school and at home. When parents adopt no style at all, it can have a detrimental effect on their children throughout their life. For example, an uninvolved parent who does little or nothing at all to support a child, emotionally or mentally, can shape a child into someone who is full of hatred, rebellion, spite and anger. These negative traits can be present throughout that child's life, and well into adulthood.

An uninvolved and unresponsive parent can also lead to a child experiencing peer pressure all too easy as there is no one at home to talk to. In turn, the child finds love and friendship with friends who he or she trusts and confides in. Some children and adolescents turn to gang culture to fill this emotional void. However, parents should be their children's confidants. They should be able to balance both roles of parent and friend and know how far to take the friendship no matter the circumstance. In any given situation, parents should be role models for their children. Children learn fast during their early years, so the earlier they are taught the quicker they retain information. This supports the concept of early childhood development being essential to achievement and success in any child's life.

HAVING A PLAN, A METHOD, A VISION

Many parents begin the parenting process without a plan, a method or vision for their children. By no means do these have to be elaborate. They just need to make sense. There are many factors about methods that help parents to implement their plans such as:

- Methods provide you with a plan and latitude to work towards your plan, ultimately achieving your goal. You may have to tweak your method at times, but it will give you the confidence needed to achieve the end result.

- Methods allow you to be focused. Even if you stray off course, your plan and system is there to remind you of your purpose.

- Methods give you a sense of stickability, assurance and stability, and show that if you are consistent you can achieve your end result.

- Methods provide interaction between parents and children. If one method does not work try to find one that does work.

How do you find a method that works? You ask around for advice or you research. Ultimately that's why you are reading this book, because you are seeking knowledge or advice. There is no single method that may work all the time. People change. Relationships change. Methods change.

STRIKING A BALANCE

Parenting must have a balance of spirituality, discipline, and unconditional love. The difficult part is finding that balance.

Parents should ensure that they are not putting their own self-interest ahead of their children's interest. For example you want them to become a doctor because you are a doctor. Or you want them to study business because you have a business degree.

Motives and intentions play an important role in striking a balance. You would not want someone leading you, or in your life, with motives and intentions that do not serve your best interest. Kostenberger and Jones indicate that: Christian parenting should be undergirded by wisdom derived from meditation on Scripture, the filling of the Holy Spirit, advice from others (this is where quality literature on parenting can be very helpful if it is balanced and based on biblical principles), and relational experience with the child.

A balance of spiritual discipline is important, as it requires wisdom and knowledge. However, knowing the kind of person you want your child to become is a determining factor in how you parent. When you equip yourself with the tools necessary to be parents, you become better positioned to be effective in your role. Planning is an essential ingredient; it requires spending time gathering resources, studying various methods, seeking guidance and direction from God in order to be effective.

There is an alarming rate of adolescents who have lost respect for their parents. Christian and moral values have been replaced with profanity and lack of respect shown by children towards their parents, guardians, family, friends, and society. Children swear at their parents, abuse and assault them; some have even killed them. It is the primary responsibility of parents to train and take care of their children and teach them to be respectful and disciplined citizens of society. However, government should also play an active role in ensuring that a good education and training is made available to both parents and children.

Over the years the family unit has not shown signs of ensuring that children are brought up with good morals. Some children in today's society are drinking alcohol with their families at social gatherings. Some children use profanity while talking to their parents, and there is no warning or rebuke. We have reached the point where children control their parents and tell them what to do instead of the parents controlling them. It appears that many families have given up on their responsibility for rearing children.

Christian morals and values have been compromised and some children seem to be beyond reproach. Many Christian parents have fallen short of being in charge and have relinquished their parental power to the child.

Parents and guardians are not the sole cause for the demise of their children's good behavior. But at the same time they are part of the problem because parents are supposed to provide training, love, direction and leadership for their children. Unfortunately, many parents have teamed up with their children in performing devious behavior and as a result, have fallen short of being called a parent. Instead of being a leader, they have become followers. Instead of providing training and love, they provide anger, and even demoralize and talk down to their children. Sadly, some parents have become a detriment to their children's very existence through toxic and unhealthy relationships.

There is a large culture of young people who have lost their way; they have no identity. Many become addicted to alcohol and drugs. Some are involved with gangs and wreak havoc on those around them. Crime is at an all-time high because of many lawless young people. Family and parents no longer have control over their children. They are unable to train up a child in the way he should go so that when he is old he may not depart. We have been given that mandate by God, especially those who take on the responsibility of having children. It is worth doing the right thing which means taking the time to train and discipline our children so we do not have to wonder whether they will choose to go down the wrong, or right, path. We all have a universal mandate as it relates to children and that is to train them.

Parents must always re-examine their position and role as a parent by asking some or all of the following questions:

1. Why am I a parent?
2. What can I provide for my child?
3. What do I want my child to become in life?
4. Do I want my child to be like me?
5. How can I assist my child in rehabilitation from drugs?
6. Should I take anger management classes?
7. Am I providing the love and affection that my child needs?
8. What am I doing wrong?
9. Can I be a better parent? How?
10. Would my parents agree with my parenting techniques?
11. Is our relationship healthy or toxic?

Compare and contrast what your parents did and what you are doing; this is important so we do not make the same mistakes. We can look at ways to improve our parenting skills regardless of whether we are parents now or plan to become parents in the future. We all have a role to play in a child's upbringing. If we as parents are not able to question ourselves, then who will question us? Who will be there to tell us we are doing something wrong? Many of us have no one to provide feedback. Who would dare tell us such a thing? If we had someone so bold, would we listen? I pose these questions for you to stop and reflect. Think about asking close friends or relatives their opinions.

Many adolescents in today's society need help. Many do not care about life, people or themselves. Gone are the days where children would not dare to hiss their teeth, or swear at their parents! Long gone are the days when a child would dare to use profanity in front of adults for fear of being disciplined by their parents when they got home. The days have vanished when young people would not dare to be seen drinking or smoking around their parents. By no means is parenting easy; it is a lifetime learning process. Once you become a parent your life is significantly altered forever, whether you like it or not. That child is a part of you forever.

The Bible says parents should *"train a child in the way he should go so that when he is old he will not depart".* (Proverbs 22:6). But how many of us really follow this advice? Many of the basic fundamental principles of good manners are not practiced anymore. Some include: *"Good morning madam/sir. Thank you. Please."*

At a very young age, my father would take me to school and I would listen to the radio program with Brother Hutch. He always inspired young listeners to have manners by reminding them of his famous quote to *"Mind your manners, because manners will take you around the whole world"*. This is still true in today's society because a child without good manners and values can potentially head in a direction that can be detrimental to their life.

You may be asking yourself what relevance or connection does good manners have to do with you, the parent or guardian, especially when it is the child you expect to have good manners. It is very relevant because you are one of the primary persons who should instill respect and good manners in your children. If they do not first respect you, then they are apt to have a difficult time respecting anyone else. The responsibility lies with you, the parent, or guardian, to teach your children and those around you how to respect you and other people. They must understand that respect is something that will take them a long way in life, like good manners. Therefore we cannot relent in directing our children in the way they should go daily.

CHAPTER 3

FUNDAMENTAL PRINCIPLES OF PARENTING

Parenting through the years can be quite a rollercoaster, but it does not have to be a nightmare. Parents can develop a bond with their children in many ways just by having regular conversations, good listening skills, and a firm demeanor. Spending quality time together and showing genuine interest in their children's hobbies, friends, and personal lives will strengthen that bond. Patience and an open mind can be helpful in making parenting years enjoyable.

Effective parenting can be achieved through the following fundamental principles:

1. Strive to live a balanced life.
2. Know when to stop working and take time out.
3. Spend time with your children.
4. Keep a watchful eye.
5. Make obedience and discipline essential.

1. Strive to live a balanced life

This is essential. Most of us are guilty of spending too much time at work trying to meet targets and not enough time with our children. One fundamental principle of parenting is having a balanced life between your job and children. Parents can easily become caught up in trying to meet work demands, deadlines and expectations. They put so much into their work until they are either too tired to spend time with their kids or they bring home work that should be left on the job. This causes a shift in their focus from the child to fulfilling work obligations. Some parents spend so much time in the office that by the time they arrive home their children are fast asleep.

2. Know when to stop working and take time out

Parents should know when to stop working and take time out for their children. They need to make it a point to shift their focus from work to their children. A day should not go by when you do not know how your child is doing. This is particularly for parents whose children live with them. It is not always easy to juggle being a parent and having a full time job, but your kids need you; so know when it's time to go home and spend time with them.

3. Spend time with your children

Spending time with your children is always a good thing although many of us lose that close bond when our children reach adolescence. But the adolescent years are when they are most susceptible to all the elements of the world such as friends, peer pressure, television, music, books, magazines, drugs and crime, etc. Some of these elements can be detrimental to them. If they decide to replace the lost time with you, it could cause them to bond with the wrong friends. When the time comes to decide whether their friends are good or bad, they become stuck in a dilemma wondering: *"Should I stick with my friend as they have proven to me that no matter what they are by my side, or should I disrespect that friend and let them go?"* If there is no bond or relationship between the parent and child, it could cause the child to choose the friend. Thus, the parent and child grow further apart.

4. Keep a watchful eye

It is helpful to adopt a proactive approach to parenting. Look for warning signs of rebellion in your children. Remember, you will never really see all of the warning signs. Do not get frustrated or angry if you miss some signs of rebellion or aggression. The key element is to recognize those signs and try to determine what is going wrong. Rebellion is a part of growing up and becoming an adolescent. It is where teenagers must try things for themselves, experience different situations and make life-altering decisions.

5. Make obedience and discipline essential

Discipline is essential in every society. Proverbs 13:24 says *"if we love our children then we discipline them. If we fail to discipline them we "hate" them"*. Proverbs 13:24 (New King James Version) says: He *who spares his rod hates his son, But he who loves him disciplines him promptly.*

Proverbs 13:11-12 (New King James Version) also says: *"My son, do not despise the chastening of the LORD, nor detest His correction; for whom the LORD loves He corrects, just as a father the son in whom he delights."*

I believe this is a model principle that everyone should follow. Now I am not telling you how you should go about disciplining your children or when to do it, but always remember that discipline is essential in the lives of our children. Do you remember when as a child growing up, your mother, father, or guardian asked you to sit down and eat your food, but all you wanted to do was go and play with your toys or friends? They told you that if you didn't eat your food you couldn't play with your toys or friends. At a very early age you learned the discipline of reasoning, because you realized that in order to go outside and play you had to listen, eat your food and obey your parents. When the light came on in your head, you immediately wanted to eat and you ate all of your food as fast as you could.

Proverbs 19:18 tells us *"Chasten your son while there is hope, And do not set your heart on his destruction."*

When you fail to discipline children and instill principles at a young age, it becomes much more difficult to instill principles at a later stage. Some parents blame everyone but themselves when they fail in disciplining their children. I have learned so much from biblical principles; they span from generation to generation. We have seen these principles tried, tested and proven. Why move away from something that works? Why abandon the principles?

Rules should be reasonable, not regulatory or arbitrary. We should be rational and fair. When disciplining our children we should ask ourselves if this is how we would want to be treated. We know that being disciplined is not a happy or pleasant occasion. We don't get joy from being disciplined but we should learn from it. Children need proper instructions and discipline early in life so that when they are old they will have respect for law and order and will obey rules and regulations. First Samuel 15:22 says: *"...to obey is better than sacrifice."*

One evening as I was driving home from work I decided to visit a friend. I arrived at a very bad time because he and his mother were having a very strong argument. They were shouting at each other, and he was using profanity. I spoke directly to my friend, letting him know that he was being disrespectful to his mom. I shared a similar situation of what I went through while living at home with my parents. I told him that sometimes you just have to ignore the situation or walk away. Then I suggested that if he increasingly found himself in the same situation of arguing then maybe he should consider moving out. I also added that he must never allow the situation to get to the point where he is shouting and swearing in the presence of his mother, even if she provoked him.

The Bible also says in Ephesians 6:4 (Good News Translation) *"Parents, do not treat your children in such a way as to make them angry. Instead, raise them with Christian discipline and instruction."* Parents are the ones who children look up to as their role models and leaders. Any provocation can bring about discouragement, discord and discomfort. If children are placed in a situation like my friend who was arguing with his mother, they should ask themselves: 'What is the most reasonable thing to do?' We should always follow God's Word by putting Him first in everything that we do. The Book of James 4:8 says *"Draw near to God and He will draw near to you. Cleanse your hands, you sinners; and purify your hearts, you double-minded."*

CHAPTER 4

BRIDGING
THE GAP

The *"generation gap"* between parents and adolescents is a reality. Times and cultures change; they bring new flavors, tastes, values and icons that define certain periods in our lives. This gap is not to be "blamed" on anyone. It is a function of normal social change. Change is that process that constantly upsets and resets the terms of everyone's existence all their lives. Cultural differences between generations are emphasized when parents identify with the old, similar, familiar, traditional, and known, while their adolescents (at a later time) become fascinated and influenced by the new, different, unfamiliar, experimental, and unknown. In most cases, the parents are culturally anchored in an earlier time and the adolescents in a later time. That is just life.

Before the internet revolution, technology was offline. However, adolescents of today are growing up in two worlds: offline and online. Thus a profound generation gap exists, even though some parents have acquired online skills in their adulthood. So how do we bridge the generation gap? Here are seven things to consider:

1. Relish the relationship.
2. Expect mistakes.
3. Spend quality time with your children.
4. Praise your children.
5. Empower your children.
6. Care for your children.
7. Communicate with your children.

1.   Relish the relationship

Relish the relationship you have with your children and build on it. Men, do not allow the fragility of your emotions to weaken your desire to be a good father. Do not say things like, *"I am too much of a man to say I love you or give my child a hug"*. Instead, initiate a conversation about how you and your child feel about one another. Far too many men believe that they should not show emotion but this belief is totally wrong. We should all know that we are loved and we should all experience unconditional love.

Do not allow the situation and circumstances surrounding you to prevent you from showing your strength and ability to provide good leadership and support for your family. Make sure you are there for your child, make sure you are there for you family, and make sure your child is attending school and has the chance to learn and achieve success. Remember to be the best you can be and stop at nothing to achieve success in your relationships with your children. Yes, there might be times when you are not able to provide the best, but you can certainly do your best.

2.   Expect mistakes

No one is perfect. Everyone makes mistakes. Far too many parents give their kids a hard time when they make mistakes. They fail to remember that they were once teenagers faced with the same problems. Some parents are harsh with their children because they do not want them to make the same mistakes they made as teenagers. The problem with this approach is that those parents can make the mistake of being too harsh and tight gripped on their children and not place enough emphasis on finding a solution to the problem.

One of the ways to combat the problem of your child hanging out with their friends who smoke or drink is to sit down and discuss why they are doing these things and talk about ways to help them stop. Yes, you might be angry and want to shout and scream at your child, but shouting and screaming does not necessarily provide a solution. Always remember that communication goes two ways, parent to child and child to parent; talk to your child so that your child will listen to you and listen to your child so that your child will talk to you.

3.   Spend quality time with your children

Spending time with your children is important but make sure it is meaningful, make sure it is quality time. The more quality time you spend the closer you become and the stronger the bond is established between you and your child. Quality time is not being with your child and talking on your cell phone or texting while together. Parents must continually ensure that they are investing in their child/children in every way possible to ensure a bright and productive future. Those ways include emotional, mental, social, financial and even physical investments. Do not think that your child is not watching you. Make sure you are giving your best in every aspect of your child's growth and development.

4.   Praise your children

Do not confuse praising your children with praising God for your children. It means to compliment your kids on their good achievements.

- Reassure them by stating that you are proud of them. If they did well on an exam or they received good grades tell them how proud you are of them and that you know they are going to do even better the next time.
- Remind them of how far they might have gone to achieve the improved grade.
- Give them something to reflect on so they can always strive to do good things on their own.

5.   Empower your children

Teach them about the Bible, life, what to expect and what not to expect. Share the "Golden Rule: Do unto other as you would have them do unto you." Matthew 7:12 says: *"So then, in everything treat others the same way you want them to treat you, for this is [the essence of] the Law and the [writings of the] Prophets.*" Remember, your kids look up to you or at least they should. Educate them about life whether it is about sex, drugs, and ways to achieve success. Empower them to emulate good role models and mentors in the world.

6.   Care for your children

Openly show them love and say you love them. It does not matter how old they may be, they still need to know that you care about them. Ask them about the things that are of their interest to show that you care and want them to succeed. If they are going on a field trip, ask whether they would like for you to join them if other parents will be there. You can show that you care by just being in their midst when they are doing things that do not involve your presence. It might be that they are packing to go on a trip. You can let them know that you care about them having the proper clothing and other items required. Maybe there is something that you can suggest that your child did not know would be needed.

7.   Communicate with your children

When children start moving from childhood to adolescence on the way to young adulthood, they begin looking for more freedom and independence; on the way to embracing their own personal expression and individuality. They want to be trusted but the only way to gain trust is through communication. Talk to your children so that you are able to gain their trust and they are able to gain yours. If there is no communication there can be no trust and if there is no trust there can be no relationship.

Communication is the key for any relationship to survive, and if truth be told, a good relationship requires good communication to survive. Communication is the social process in which two or more parties exchange information and share meaning (G. Moorhead et al., 2000 p.196). We communicate with our children to achieve a result; to share information.

Families share information about paying bills, taking the children to school, performance in school, dinner and so on. They also give directions related to specific tasks. For example, some parents tell their children that it is time to wash the dishes, time to do their homework or it is time to go to bed. These directions establish who is in charge.

Communication is not just used to inform others, it is used to foster understanding, to explain, clarify or enforce a rule. We communicate to express the way we feel. Whether it is expressing love towards our children, displeasure, confidence or anger, we all express our emotions.

- Communication between a parent and child is vital in order to make decisions, talk about alternative solutions and to achieve effective results.
- Communication establishes a bond between parent and child.

Without communication there can be no solution because there is no exchanging of information in order to bring about a result. If Jesus had not communicated with His Father where would we be today?

"I am the way, the truth, and the life. No one comes to the Father except through me." John 14:6. The "way" signifies the path. The truth signifies that there is no other. Jesus is the only truth. The life signifies our very existence. Having life

allows us to live. We are dead without life. "No one" is self-explanatory. There is no other way but through Jesus that we have access to the father.

- He died to save our sins and was resurrected.
- He can be seen as the way to the Father.
- He can be seen as the truth because He is the revelation of God and life.
- He communicates to God on our behalf (Radmacher, E. 1999, p.1346).

Without Jesus we cannot communicate with God. Through Jesus we have access to the Father whereby we are able to talk to Him and share our emotions and feelings. However, in order to speak to the Father we must establish a personal relationship with Jesus. The relationship that Jesus has with His Father can be seen as a model that parents can use with their children. Jesus is able to speak to His Father and even question Him.

When communicating with your children, request feedback from them after having communicated your feelings, views and the reason you made your decisions. For example, ask your child how he or she feels about the decision made or about the situation at hand. Feedback is crucial as you can use it to correct mistakes. You can also use feedback to ensure that you don't make the same mistake again.

Parents should communicate with their children by spending the same time and effort they use to communicate with their friends or even more. This would definitely change your relationship with them. They should be careful not to discredit their children when communicating to them. This can be done by speaking negatively to them or about them.

Effective communication should focus on getting the attention of your children. That means the information you present should be appealing. What you say should catch their attention. Presentation is important. You would not want someone to give you a dull or boring speech or presentation and neither do they; this causes them to lose focus and interest.

Bridging the gap requires parents to watch for first impressions as they are usually the lasting ones. Parents should be careful that the counsel given is wise and proportionate to the result they are trying to achieve.

Furthermore, you tend to find that if an option is given and that option can help them get what they want, teens usually reconsider and make the unwise choices which can be detrimental to them.

People tend to shut down when a presentation is aggressive or no explanation is given to a conclusion. Therefore presentation and effective communication can make a relationship so much easier. Your presentation matters. How you conduct yourself matters.

Along with communication should be the goal of reconciliation. The objective is to reconcile any differences in order to obtain a positive outcome. One interesting point Horne makes is that often we make quick judgments in conflicts. We should not forget to acknowledge our own sins (Horne p67, para2). It is amazing how many times we don't recognize that we can be the problem to conflict. However we tend not to notice our own misfortunes or issues. But we must remember that we are trying to reconnect any disconnect. Where possible we are trying to be proactive and not retroactive.

Horne indicates that when initially communicating with an angry teen you should listen so you can "draw out what is deep within". Your job is not to fix, interrogate, dictate or bring salvation. This is important because there are times when some people come into a conversation either upset or they try to fix the problem without really taking the time to listen and digest what is being said. This can create confusion, empathy and annoyance for a teen already upset. You are not a police interrogator. You do not work for the Secret Service. It is okay to ask questions. It may not be okay to conduct a full scale interrogation interview. Parents should be bridging gaps and building bonds.

How do we bridge a gap that is broken and build a bond that may never have been there? Here are five things that you can do:

a)   Listen.

b)   Trust.

c)   Be logical and practical.

d)   Ask how they feel or what they think.

e)   Embrace change.

While attempting to bridge gaps, we must remember that we cannot change a person. Only God can. This is where prayer comes in. We must pray without ceasing. Many times we pray but our prayer is not answered because we pray once and stop. Or we get tired of praying. But God knows our heart and our desires.

CHAPTER 5

GENERATIONAL CYCLES

Have you ever looked at your parents and said to yourself: *"Wow, I sound exactly like them! Oh wow, I yawn just like my dad! Wow, I laugh just like my mother; I don't have any patience just like my father!"* Have you ever looked at the relationship between you and your parents and said: *"Wow, this is why I don't like a lot of people! This is why I am an introvert and keep things within my heart."*

We must remember that bad parenting skills can have detrimental effects on children (Nelson Commentary, p.976). Likewise, good parenting skills produce positive effects. Therefore the things we do and say can affect our children and their children's children. Parents should ask themselves this question: *"Would I want my child to grow up doing the things I am doing right now or have done in the past?"* You may have taken drugs, or you may have been an adulterer; you may have been involved in an abusive relationship. We know that generational cycles are possible.

Some men do not always know how to be good fathers, and some sons do not know how to be good sons. Perhaps one of the reasons is because we do not take the time to communicate and understand each other as men. Sometimes as sons we have this image that our dads are perfect. No one ever tells us differently. As a child, who would say that your dad is imperfect, a dead beat or horrible? As sons we should respect our father's struggles, weaknesses, needs and faults. We should try to understand why our fathers are the way they are. They have to deal with issues at work, and then come home to their family making sure food is on the table and the bills are paid. He also has to manage the family home as well as making sure that the marital home is in order first. The same can be said for some mothers.

Many of us regurgitate what our fathers did. Many hold on to anger, hate and hurt. But this does not have to be the case. A father's toxic traits may have a detrimental effect on his future generations. So the question that you may be asking is: *How do we stop toxic generational cycles?* A starting point would be to seek professional help from a counselor or therapist. We should also pray because prayer changes things. Prayer is powerful and can be very effective.

This is illustrated throughout the bible. Prayer is a remedy for sickness, pain or malady. We should be precise about what we want God to do in our lives. If we want Him to help us break a generational cycle we should tell Him.

In 2 Samuel 14:25, David's son Absalom was handsome and charming; he was the most handsome man in all of Israel. Absalom was influential and ambitious in that he was the son of David and enjoyed all of his father's royal privileges. 2 Samuel chapters 15 and 16 reveal how Absalom was influential enough to start a revolt against his father. He loved power and even slept with his father's concubine.

Perhaps promiscuity was one of the generational struggles passed on from David to Absalom. But this does not have to be you because you can choose the direction for your life; you are the captain of your ship. You are the author of your own life. You don't have to allow the toxic traits of your father to enshrine and define you. His sins do not have to be accepted by you. The harmful consequences of his life do not have to resonate in yours.

We have the power, ability, and right to break every cycle that is prohibiting us or passed down through our forefathers. It can be done through our prayers (1 Thessalonians 5:17). This is why it is so important to understand that faith without works is dead because action is always needed. Until you decide to act on what has you in bondage, you will never receive your release.

Parents should cover their children in prayer and pray with them. Prayer is like a spiritual blanket and when praying for your children it keeps them protected. But prayer is not a guarantee from pain, hardships, troubles or suffering. Exodus chapter 32 reveals how God threatened to wipe out the children of Israel. Moses prayed and asked Him not to do so. God answered his prayer. Elijah prayed earnestly that it would not rain and it did not rain. He then prayed again and it rained!

Prayer is our secret weapon. We must use it to cover our children. We must pray effectively and efficiently. We must pray with a purpose.

We must pray that our children connect with the right peers, and that they will become generational movers and shakers. Pray that they will be effective children of God who will use their gifts and talents to glorify Him. Don't just pray that God will keep them safe, but pray that they will impact a nation and change future generations! We are praying for the past, the present and the future for our children. Pray for God's favor to cover them and go before them.

In, 2nd Samuel 18:33 Nathan then said to David, *"And the king was much moved, and went up to the chamber over the gate, and wept: and as he went, thus he said, O my son Absalom, my son, my son Absalom! would God I had died for thee, O Absalom, my son, my son!"*

David grieved at what his sin had opened the door to in his own family. Probably, like Esau, he sought to take it back with tears, but to no avail. The deed was done, the consequences would follow. David was an indulgent parent. David opened the door to affliction on this family when he slept with Bathsheba and murdered Uriah. David's own sinful indulgence of his passions and rebellions against God, were seen in his sons. David's pain and hurt show us that it isn't enough that parents train their children to be godly; they must first train themselves in godliness. Whatever you allow to enter your door affects everyone in the family. I don't think David or Ghazi had any idea what was lurking behind the door they opened. I don't think they fully understood what the consequences of their actions could be. As a result of David's actions God said in 2 Samuel 12:10, *"Now therefore the sword shall never depart from thine house; because thou hast despised me, and hast taken the wife of Uriah the Hittite to be thy wife."*

David was the sweet Psalmist of Israel. He was the apple of God's eye; he was the king, whose throne was forever established, and yet he brought down a curse, that was not just for three or four generations, but that would never depart from his house.

You may be wondering who did what in your genealogy. Are they the cause of you having children out of wedlock, a drug habit, alcohol addiction, or financial problems? Generational cycles mean sins of the parents can have negative results in future generations. People sometimes say if your father was an alcoholic the chances are that you will also become an alcoholic. I may not be able to prove it but I think the cycle on David's family ended at Calvary. He lived under the Old Covenant, and we live under the New Covenant. When a man or woman opens their heart, home, and life to Christ, the blessing is far greater than any cycle that comes through the fall of man, or the sins of your ancestors.

Romans 8:2 says, *"For the law of the Spirit of life in Christ Jesus has set you free from the law of sin and of death."*

The law of sin and death is two-fold:

1. The wages of sin is death.
2. The wages of sin is that they are often passed down to following generations.

What Christ did, eclipses what Adam did. The life in Christ is greater than the death in Adam. So if you are concerned about what your grandfather did then you are putting yourself under the Old Covenant. Jesus passes on blessings that far surpass and remove any curse that may have entered through your family lineage. The law of the spirit of life in Christ Jesus swallows up the law of sin and death that grandpa may have released into your family. When a light is turned on in a dark room it completely overpowers the darkness, just as the spirit of life in Christ Jesus overpowers any generational cycle that would have been passed down.

Romans 5:15-17 The Message (MSG) Translation
"Yet the rescuing gift is not exactly parallel to the death-dealing sin. If one man's sin put crowds of people at the dead-end abyss of separation from God, just think what God's gift poured through one man, Jesus Christ, will do! There's no comparison between that death-dealing sin and this generous, life-giving gift. The verdict on that one sin was the death sentence; the verdict on the many sins that followed was this wonderful life sentence. If death got the upper hand through one man's wrongdoing, can you imagine the breath-taking recovery life makes, sovereign life, in those who grasp with both hands this wildly extravagant life-gift, this grand setting-everything-right that the one man Jesus Christ provides?"

CHAPTER 6
LOVE

Matthew 22:35-40 states, *"One of them, an expert in the law, tested him with this question: "Teacher, which is the greatest commandment in the Law?" Jesus replied: "'Love the Lord your God with all your heart and with all your soul and with all your mind.' This is the first and greatest commandment. And the second is like it: 'Love your neighbor as yourself.' All the Law and the Prophets hang on these two commandments."*

The greatest thing you can do is to love. In the famous love chapter of the Bible, 1 Corinthians 13, it says that faith, hope, and love are present, but the greatest is love. Once we respond to God's love for us and begin to love Him back, we find that we are also able to love the other people in our lives.

Loving God is what we were made for, yet sometimes it seems like we don't even come close to really knowing Him or loving Him.

"We love because he first loved us."

1 John 4:19 (New International Version)

And yet just being loved by God is not enough. We must receive His love and allow it to change us. Then we become capable of the kind of love that comes from Him!

"This is love: not that we loved God, but that he loved us and sent his Son as an atoning sacrifice for our sins."

1 John 4:10

Sin and selfishness rob us of our ability to love. But when we receive God's love and what He did for us through Jesus and His death on a cross, it changes us. One would think that loving your family would be the easiest thing to do. Yet, we find families that do not seem to love one another. The Bible says a lot about family relationships and love. Let's take a look together at some of them:

"Honour thy father and thy mother: that thy days may be long upon the land which the Lord thy God giveth thee."

Exodus 20:12

"Children's children are the crown of old men, And the glory of children is their father."
Proverbs 17:6

"If someone says, "I love God," and hates his brother, he is a liar; for he who does not love his brother whom he has seen, how can he love God whom he has not seen?"
1 John 4:20

"And you, fathers, do not provoke your children to wrath, but bring them up in the training and admonition of the Lord."
Ephesians 6:4

"A wise son makes a glad father, But a foolish son is the grief of his mother."
Proverbs 10:1

"Husbands, love your wives, just as Christ loved the church and gave himself up for her."
Ephesians 5:25 (New International Version)

Wives, submit to your husbands as to the Lord.

Ephesians 5:22

"He who loves his wife loves himself."

Ephesians 5:28

"A wife must respect her husband."

Ephesians 5:33

Families should be showing love, respect, honor, and obedience. But we see and sometimes live quite the opposite. If we want to change, then we have to go back to loving God. When we receive His love for us, it changes us and teaches us to love unselfishly.

When we learn to love by receiving God's love, we begin to realize that there is no room for selfishness in our hearts. So instead of fighting, arguing, demanding, pushing, and striving for our own way, we must honor the Lord by showing love towards others; including family.

"But now you must rid yourselves of all such things as these: anger, rage, malice, slander, and filthy language from your lips. Do not lie to each other, since you have taken off your old self with its practices and have put on the new self, which is being renewed in knowledge in the image of its Creator." Colossians 3:8-10

"Therefore, as God's chosen people, holy and dearly loved, clothe yourselves with compassion, kindness, humility, gentleness and patience. Bear with each other and forgive whatever grievances you may have against one another. Forgive as the Lord forgave you. And over all these virtues put on love, which binds them all together in perfect unity." Colossians 3:12-14

This is how you can love your family! Love Yourself. Sometimes we can get so down on ourselves for our failures and weaknesses that we begin to base our identity and our sense of value on our worst moments when we fail miserably. God wants to change that false sense of identity in us. He wants us to begin to see ourselves the way He does.

Quite often people tend to treat others the way they feel about themselves. If they do not like who they are and fail to see the value of God's image within them, then they will pass that negativity on to everyone around them. When we allow Him to change us and help us become who He created us to be, then we begin to see the whole world in a new light! So here are four crucial keys to implement in your life:

- Love God;
- Love your neighbor;
- Love your family; and
- Love yourself.

You should live in love. You should eat, sleep, walk and drink love. Your actions should show love. Your thoughts and responses should be based on love. Let love be the template you use to represent God because God is love. The same applies to parenting. One of the greatest gifts you can give to your children is love.

- Love creates a bond between a parent and child unlike no other.
- Love makes up for any inefficiencies you may have as a parent.

- Love creates and builds relationships.
- Love builds bonds.

Where there is love there are no limits or boundaries. Parents should show love to their children. Physically express their love to them. Mentally and emotionally express your love to them. Verbally express your love to them.

Family love involves a special bond that should always be protected. Each family member may be different, but there is an unconditional love that exists among them. You should also love your brothers and sisters in Christ the same way. They are your spiritual family. Romans 12:9-10 (New International Version) says *"Love must be sincere. Hate what is evil; cling to what is good. Be devoted to one another in brotherly love."*

Many of us have perfected the art of pretending to love and show interest. However, God wants us to be sincere and genuine in our love. Genuine and sincere love involves being real. Parenting encompasses all of this and more. This kind of love should also be reflected in parenting and makes children feel safe and secure.

One of the reasons we see many young people turning to gangs is because of the lack of loving oneself and also a lack of parents showing love and providing love in the home. We have children who turn to gangs that provide them with a sense of love. The seeds we sow with our parents can potentially determine the seeds we will sow and reap with our children. This truly impacts the parent-child relationship. If we have any anger, malice or resentment towards our parents then we should repent to God.

Love should be shown towards everyone. Love brings people together. Love soothes rage and anger. Love breaks down walls. Where communication is broken love provides trust and confidence. Love provides for a change to occur. Jesus tells us over and over that we should love one another. Love is documented throughout scripture. We must always remember that God is love and if we say we love God then we must love each other. How can we love God if we cannot love our parents, our friends, our family and our enemies? Love is the only way.

For God so loved the world that He gave His only begotten Son, that whoever believes in Him should not perish but have everlasting life. John 3:16

God loves us so much that He gave us His only son Jesus Christ so that we could have the opportunity to be saved and go to heaven. So you must not only love others but the Bible takes it even further and says that you shall love others as yourselves. God first says that He wants us to love Him with everything we have and then turn around and love others the same way we love ourselves.

Then God says to love even your enemies. Yes, the people who may dislike you, people you may see as your opposition, and the people who do not love you. This is who God is. He wants us to love Him and all others. He loves each of us and there are no exceptions.

God wants us to love everyone with no exceptions, limits or boundaries. If we love God we should keep His commandments. It is through keeping His commandments that we show our love for God.

In John 14:21, Jesus says *"He who has My commandments and keeps them, it is he who loves Me. And he who loves Me will be loved by My Father, and I will love him and manifest Myself to him. We should obey God's Word and keep His commandments. Without love you profit nothing."*

"Without love the gifts God has given you are nothing. The good things you do without love amount to nothing. Love is everlasting. Love never fails." 1 Corinthians 13:1-3

CHAPTER 7
HONOR

The noun "Honor" (i.e. the Lord is worthy of all Honor) is that which is paid in token of worth or value, worship, dignity, an estimate (written or spoken) of worth or an appraisal. The adjective (i.e. Honored guest) means valuable, precious, of great worth, respected, and held in high regard. Honor has to do with acknowledging the value of a person or thing and affirming or convening that value by word or deed.

There are really two parts to honoring:

1. Acknowledge Value
This part has to do with what happens in our own thinking. It is something we choose to do. It is a decision we make regarding people and even things. Here, the focus is on people. This thought process has two aspects:

a. Assign or ascribe value

We chose to assign or ascribe value and honor regardless of a person's demonstrated value. This is done all the time. We can choose to treat people with respect, esteem them, their ideas, their contribution to society and even their place in our own life. We can assign or ascribe value in spite of actual behavior.

The second aspect of acknowledging value has to do with adjusting our perspective.

b. Apprehend value

We look through the eyes of God seeking worth and value. Every person, in some way, bears the image of his or her Creator. When it comes to people, we make a decision to treasure or value them because God tells us to do so, and at their very core they actually still bear the image of our Lord and Master.

Honoring people begins in our own perceptions of them. We came from the same Creator. When we dis-Honor others we dis-Honor the one who made them. Honoring is a choice to advance people on a value scale.

All of us have developed criteria by which we evaluate the worth of a person or thing. Honoring is a choice to retool our criteria to match God's eternal perspective and to deliberately move people up on our scale of importance.

2. Affirm Value

At some time, the value we apprehend or ascribe in our thinking and attitude toward others must be affirmed to the person Honored by some word or deed. Honoring someone must move from acknowledgment to affirmation. Love that is concealed does little for the one being loved. Honor that we fail to communicate does little to encourage the one being honored. Honor is communicated by words and deeds. Just as we can love and Honor one another in word and deed, we can also devalue one another by our deeds and words. Valuing begins in the mind and devaluing and dishonor begin in our thinking.

God holds the parent-child relationship as special. God tells us in the Ten Commandments to obey and have respect for our parents. The Bible tells parents that they should respect their children and not provoke them. The parent-child relationship is one of truth and Honor. The same relationship that God desires of us as God's children is the same relationship that we should have with our children. Parents should be the source of wisdom and every good thing for their children.

Ephesians 6:1-4 says *"Children, obey your parents in the Lord, for this is right. "Honor your father and mother"-- which is the first commandment with a promise-- "that it may go well with you and that you may enjoy long life on the earth." Fathers, do not exasperate your children; instead, bring them up in the training and instruction of the Lord."* There are two elements to this command:

a. The first element is children, Honor your parents.

i. What does God mean when He says to Honor your father and mother?

ii. The answer to that question is found in the Hebrew word *Kavod* translated as "Honor." It literally means "heavy or weighty."

The word "heavy" designates importance or stature. To Honor your parents means to give them a position of respect and importance in your life. There is no time limit on this command. Like the others, it stays in force for our entire lives.

b. The second element is parents, be honorable. God wants parents to serve as models of faithful obedience to his principles and demonstrate what it means to live in relationship with him. In today's society there's not a more difficult task than being a parent. One man said: "There was a time when I had six theories about raising children but didn't have any children. Now I have six children and no theories."

God's 5th Commandment does not say, "Honor your parents if you think they deserve it." This commandment to Honor is in force totally apart from the way parents perform. You may have had lousy parents; unfortunately many children grow up with parents who are absent, or abusive, or cruel. However, you should still show Honor.

Your parents may have separated or gotten a divorce and remarried when you were very young. One or both of your parents may have had a drinking or drug problem. Any of these issues could have affected your relationship with your parents. However, your parents' failure in parenting does not excuse you from obeying the 5th Commandment that says "Honor your father and mother."

The way your parents performed may affect your relationship with them and it will certainly affect the way you obey this commandment and the motivation you bring to the task. But it does not affect the reality that you must obey it regardless of their quality of parenting.

Deuteronomy 5:16 (New King James Version) says) *"Honor your father and your mother, as the LORD your God has commanded you, that your days may be long, and that it may be well with you in the land which the LORD your God is giving you."*

Children honoring parents is associated with the benefits of long life and success.

Matthew 15:4 (New King James Version)) says *"For God commanded, saying, 'Honor your father and your mother' and, 'He who curses father or mother, let him be put to death."*

When God issued this commandment to Moses on Mount Sinai, He demonstrated His sovereign plan for real relationships. God demands all who have been brought into a personal relationship with Him to Honor Him. And just as we are to Honor the One who created us, so we are to Honor our fathers and mothers who were chosen to carry out God's plan for our creation. Nonetheless, there are children who hurt deeply because of various kinds of parental abuse. Yet God designed parent-child relationships to be among the most vital of all human relationships. This may be why He spoke not only of Honor, but also attached the promise of "long life" to His command in Exodus 20:12 *"Honor your father and your mother, that your days may be long upon the land which the Lord your God is giving you."*

In Proverbs 6:20-23, God's Word tells us to pay attention to our fathers and to listen to our mothers. We are to hold their instructions in our hearts and tie them around our necks. In return, we receive guidance, protection, teaching and discipline—four ingredients no one can afford to live without.

The promise of a long life is the promise of God's lifelong protection, guidance, deliverance and provision. So Honor your God-given responsibility because God commands it.

It is important to understand that some people may not have the best parents. In fact, some parents may be toxic. Thus, many might struggle to honor a mother or father who is seen in this regard. Honoring them becomes even harder when there is no relationship or not much of a relationship or when the relationship often elicits hurt or pain. So how can we still honor our parents if they are toxic, if there is no relationship, or if they bring about sadness or pain? Here are a few ways to honor them:

1. Show honor

This can be done by showing love or appreciation through presenting a nice gift, giving a compliment, or commending the person. In essence, what you are trying to do is sift through the mess, issues or pain to find ways to be grateful, respectful, and appreciative. We give honor because someone has earned it because it is the right thing to do, we give honor to show respect, and we give honor to set an example.

Note to parents: If you, as a parent, are always scolding, belittling or showing disrespect toward your own mother or father, you encourage your own children to follow such harsh and insolent behavior. If you're dishonoring authority, you're setting a precedent and pattern for dishonoring authority in your home. Instead, in being a parent, you should model honesty and honor, so that your children will learn the same. Lead by positive example so that your children can follow suit!

2. Be forgiving

God has given us the gift of forgiveness and we have the ability to share that gift with your parents. I am in no way encouraging you to excuse or invite their sin, nor am I encouraging you to allow yourself or loved ones to be subjected to harm or hurt. What I am encouraging you to do is to release parents who have wronged you in any way. In releasing them, you can rid yourself of any animosity or bitterness you may have towards them. You can also release any debt that you believe they owe you. Let it go! Let it go so you can grow! Do not allow yourself to be the judge of the situation but hand the issue to the supreme judge: Jesus. Once you forgive and release the person who has hurt you or caused you pain, it begins the process of healing, growth, and moving forward.

Through honoring your parents, your heart softens and opens to the possibility of giving and receiving forgiveness. Forgiveness provides you the opportunity to become emotionally healthy and to overcome the pain and hurt that you may have from the past. Further, forgiveness allows you to open the door to having a healthier relationship with your parents if possible. If you are a parent, through forgiveness you can stop the generational pain or generational cycle that may have been passed down through your lineage. You can start a new loving and caring family lineage that shows honor, love, and respect without holding a grudge, animosity or hate. Remember healing comes through forgiveness.

3. Be gracious

Remember God has shown us a lot of grace, which is a gift we can also give to our parents. We have the ability to love our enemies, this includes the parents who hurt us. Be gracious, kind and loving towards them. If you are gracious towards them and show love, you are treating them the way God treats us. When our parents see this outward love shown to them, sometimes this might potentially lead to their own repentance. The book of Romans tells us that it's the kindness of God that leads us to repentance, as within God's grace, we are inspired to recognize how far from grace we really are. The aim is not to be self-righteous. The aim is to be gracious and show grace and love and pray that eventually our parents' hearts would soften and change because of this.

WE ARE TO HONOR OTHER PEOPLE

"...what are mere mortals that you should think about them, human beings that you should care for them? Yet you made them only a little lower than God and crowned them with glory and honor." Psalm 8:4-5

We are to Honor each other. We are to recognize the great value that God has placed on humanity. The word tells us here that people have been crowned with great Honor. Not just the rich people, the intelligent people, the talented people, but all mortals, all human beings.

Above all authorities and relationships, we are to Honor God. We do this two different ways:

1.   **The first is with our bodies**

"...for God bought you with a high price. So you must honor God with your body." 1 Corinthians 6:20 (New International Version).

God places great value upon himself and his Son. God is valuable and He realizes it. He tells us that He is the Creator of everything. He is in control of everything around us. He paid a high price so you can Honor Him by service and righteous living.

2.   **The second way we Honor God is with our giving**

"Honor the Lord with your wealth and with the best part of everything you produce." Proverbs 3:9 (New International Version).

"So humble yourselves under the mighty power of God, and at the right time he will lift you up in honor." 1 Peter 5:6 (New International Version).

CONCLUSION

Today's society has become very complex and challenging for parents and families to provide structure and core values for their children and adolescents. With any approach to values and morals comes a new way of thinking because many parents are departing from traditional ways of parenting while adapting to change; many need to first see the change in order to change. Some parents need to take on a new mindset and vision of parenthood.

This book has provided keys about parenting to impacting the next generation with a focus on family and parenting. You have received some basic principles to assist in effective training and parenting adolescents and all children. Several parenting styles were discussed along with the serious effects that some styles have on the developmental outcome of children and adolescents. Emphasis was placed on the importance of parents and families being able to strike a balance especially in their discipline and spirituality.

There is no mandatory list of things that reveal how parenting should be done. Instead you have received keys to help parents in fulfilling God's purpose for His family. Patience and an open mind can be helpful in making these years of childhood and adolescence enjoyable.

While there is no one method of parenting, there are different approaches that come together to achieve a better result to parenting. Family has a tremendous effect on the socialization of children and adolescents. They must take on the overall responsibility to guide them, show them right from wrong, discipline them and try their very best to lead them in the right direction.

Furthermore we should all consider what type of parents we are and what style of parenting we possess. We should assess how we can become better and more effective parents. Parents should never forget to balance their role of parenting with their daily jobs, tasks, or whatever it is they have to do. Avoid isolating your children because you are too busy to spend time with them or communicate with them. The key is to provide good communication if you want to have a healthy relationship.

The things children go through in their homes, whether good or bad, can affect them for the rest of their lives. Finally, as adults we must set examples for our kids by showing them respect and love, and by honoring them. Children are a blessing from God and should be treated as such. Whenever we are in doubt about how to love them, we should always follow the example that Christ has shown us.

One thing to remember is that we are a product of our environment. I use 'we' collectively because it extends to our parents, family, leaders and includes me. We determine who we will become and where we end up in life by the decisions we make. But most importantly, you and I decide where we will end up in life. Helen Keller didn't allow her blindness to stop her from achieving success. She didn't allow her environment, society or situation to prohibit her from reading and writing. Forest Gump was a child who could not walk. He was talked about and teased at school. They even threw shoes at him. But Forest did not allow others to stop him from making progress in life. He went to college, played football, met the President of the United States and traveled. He graduated and received a degree and eventually joined the army.

If only we all had the courage and faith to believe that we could overcome our most difficult obstacle. Both Helen and Forest went through a process of self-development. For some, the process of self-development may be lengthy, but the end result can be life changing.

Today's parents and families must not give up the fight to impact their next generation. We must build our society without straying away from the basic fundamentals of parenting. A plethora of young people have emerged and begun to self-destruct because of their inability to develop themselves. They are not able to shift! Many children and adolescents are failing because they are ill-equipped to deal with today's challenges and pressures of life in their homes, neighborhoods, schools and society. If we can conquer our mind and the way we think about our inabilities, imperfections and even disabilities, like Forest Gump and Helen Keller, we can overcome our greatest challenges and live a successful life.

BIBLIOGRAPHY

BOOKS

Gage. *Canadian Concise Dictionary*. (2002). Toronto: Gage Educational Publishing Company.

Gordon, Michael. *The Nuclear Family in Crisis: The Search for an Alternative*. 1972. New York: Harper & Row.

Horne, Rick. *Get Outta My Face*. 2009. Wapwallopen, PA: Shepherd Press.

Kostenberger, J. Andreas, Jones, W. David. GOD, *Marriage and Family*. 2010. Illinois: Crossway.

Moorhead, G. et al. *Organizational Behavior*. 2000. Boston, Massachusetts: Houghton Mifflin Company. Moorhead, G. et al.2000.

Munroe, Myles. *The Purpose And Power of Love & Marriage.* 2002. Shippensburg, PA: Destiny Image Publishers, Inc.

Munroe, M. (January 2015). *The Principles and Power of Vision: Keys to Achieving Personal and Corporate Destiny.* New Kensington, PA: Whitaker House.

Shaffer, R. D. *Development Psychology Childhood & Adolescence.* 1999. California: Brooks/Cole Publishing Company.

Siegler, R. et al. *How Children Develop.* 2003. New York: Worth Publishers. The Holy Bible (NIV) (2011 ed.). Grand Rapids, MI: Zondervan. al, D. e. (1985).

JOURNAL ARTICLES

Aldous J, Mulligan G. "Father's child care and children's behavioral problems." *J Family Issues* 2002; 23:624-47.

Barber, Nigel. "Single Parenthood As A Predictor of Cross-National Variation in Violent Crime." *Cross-Cultural Research Vol. 38,* (November 2004): 343-358.

Bremberg S, Kristiansson R, Oberklaid F, Sarkadi A. "Fathers' Involvement and Children's Developmental Outcomes: A Systematic Review of Longitudinal Studies" 2007; 153-158.

Coleman WL, Garfield C, and the Committee on Psychosocial Aspects of Child and Family Health. "Fathers and Pediatricians: enhancing men's roles in the care and development of their children." *Pediatrics* 2004; 113: 1406-11.

Harris K, Marmer J. "Poverty, paternal involvement, and adolescent well-being". *J Family Issues* 1996; 17: 614-40; Harris K, Furstenberg F, Marmer J. "Paternal involvement with adolescents in intact families: The influence of fathers over the life course." *Demography* 1998; 35: 201-16.

Teachman, Jay, et al. "Sibling Resemblance in Behavioral and Cognitive Outcomes: The Role of Father Presence." *Journal of Marriage and the Family* Vol. 60, (Nov 1998): 835-848.

Vaden-Kiernan N, Ialongo N, Pearson J, et al. "Household family structure and children's aggressive behavior: A longitudinal study of urban elementary school children." *J Abnormal Child Psychology* 1995; 23: 553-68.

STATISTICS

United States Department of Health and Human Services.

National Centre for Health Statistics. Survey on Child Health. Washington, D.C.: GPO.1993.

U.S. Department of Health and Human Services. National Center for Health Statistics. Survey on Child Health. Washington, D.C.: GPO, 1993.

www.ingramcontent.com/pod-product-compliance
Lightning Source LLC
LaVergne TN
LVHW011337080426
835513LV00006B/400